D1175213

Bouquet de
BOURGOGNE

On this side of the town the ground rises sharply towards a rocky crest, crowned by the ruins of a feudal fortress – a dismantled castle, whose solid keep has alone defied the power of Marazin. A steep path, deeply worn in the rock, winds upwards. A wrinkled sibyl, distaff in hand, herds the solitary goat which browses on the scanty herbage of its banks; a bare-headed, bare-footed girl, knitting as she goes, marshals her flock of geese with a switch; a priest, with half-shut eyes and his thumb in his closed breviary, repeats his midday prayers, as he follows its windings, courting the line of diapered shadow which the plane trees cast upon the path. So far as human voices go, it is a silent spot, from which the traveller, seated among the ruined walls, looks down on the town nestling below the hill and encircled by the river. All around, the air is resonant with the chatter of jackdaws, the hum of insects, and the chirrup of grasshoppers.

R.E. PROTHERO,
The Pleasant Land of France 1908

Bouquet de
BOURGOGNE

SEASONAL RECIPES
FROM LA CÔTE ST JACQUES, JOIGNY

Michel and Jean-Michel Lorain

Illustrations by
Nadine Wickenden

PAVILION

First published in Great Britain in 1994 by
Pavilion Books Limited
26 Upper Ground, London SE1 9PD

Recipes copyright © 1994 by
Michel and Jean-Michel Lorain
Illustrations copyright © 1994 by
Nadine Wickenden

Designed by Janet James

A CIP catalogue record for this book is
available from the British Library

ISBN 1-85793-396-6

Printed and bound in Hong Kong by
Imago Publishing

2 4 6 8 10 9 7 5 3 1

This book may be ordered by post direct from
the publisher. Please contact the Marketing
Department. But try your bookshop first.

Contents

The fertile and rich countryside of rural Burgundy reawakens in spring after a winter which is often biting and harsh. From Auxerre to Mâcon, the slumbering countryside is beginning to blossom in every corner of the region, from the gently rolling vine-clad hillsides and the national park of Morvan to the banks of the fish-filled river Saône. Spring is the best season for sharing in the artistry and *joie de vivre* that Burgundy has cultivated for hundreds of years. From the market stalls and gourmands' tables rise the evocative aromas of market-garden produce and wild mushrooms, and fresh asparagus is prominent on every stall. The carefully tended vineyards and orchards are all in flower, and the long hours of sunshine dispel any lingering worries of the wine-growers, who are justly proud of their lively white wines and their well-rounded reds. The diversity of these wines allows them to be adapted to every culinary preparation: perch, pike, snails, frogs' legs, organic meats and the first red fruits. This spring landscape is associated in Burgundy with a cuisine which is traditional and faithful to its rich soil yet which reflects the creative fantasy of the season.

MENUS

Warm Salad of Lobster and Vegetables
*Homard tiède sur petites salades
maraîchères*

Traditional Burgundy Beef Stew
*Boeuf bourguignon traditionnel au
vin d'Irancy*

Asparagus with Truffle Butter
Asperges vertes au beurre de truffe

Triple-Tiered Chocolate Mousse
Gâteau au chocolat noir

———————

Frogs' Legs with Broad (Fava) Beans and
Morel Mushrooms
*Cassolette de grenouilles, fèves vertes
et morilles*

Shepherd's Pie with Epoisse Cheese and
Garlic Sauce
*Le parmentier d'agneau au fromage
d'Epoisse sauce à l'ail*

Seasonal Vegetables with Wild
Mushroom Mousseline Sauce
*L'assiette de légumes à la mousseline de
champignons des bois*

Apple and Black Currant Parcels
with Cinnamon
*La papillote de pommes et cassis à
la cannelle*

**S
P
R
I
N
G**

WARM SALAD OF LOBSTER AND VEGETABLES

Homard tiède sur petites salades maraîchères

SERVES 4

4 small live lobsters, about 350g/12oz each
2 tbsp white wine vinegar
$^1/_2$ tsp Dijon mustard
salt and pepper
6 tbsp extra virgin olive oil
100g/3$^1/_3$oz white mushrooms, stems
trimmed
juice of $^1/_2$ lemon
100g/3$^1/_3$oz French green beans, topped and tailed
500ml/16fl oz/2 cups lobster sauce (see below)
30g/1oz/2 tbsp butter, cut in pieces
100g/3$^1/_3$oz mixed salad greens, washed
and dried

FOR THE LOBSTER SAUCE
1 small carrot, peeled and chopped
$^1/_2$ onion, peeled and chopped
$^1/_2$ stick celery, chopped
30g/1oz/2 tbsp butter
4 lobster heads, roughly chopped
45ml/3 tbsp Cognac
250ml/8fl oz/1 cup dry white wine
1 large tomato, roughly chopped
30g/1oz/2 tbsp tomato paste
1 clove garlic, peeled and crushed
750ml/1$^1/_4$ pints/3 cups fish stock or water
1 bouquet garni
10 black peppercorns, crushed

Rinse the lobsters and cook them in a large pot of simmering water for 8 minutes. Remove the heads to use in
the lobster sauce. Crack the claws and gently pull out the
meat, keeping the claw shape intact. Gently remove the
tail meat from the shell, keeping the tail fans as decoration for the plate. Reserve about 500ml/16fl oz/2 cups of
the cooking liquid. Cover all the lobster and set aside.

To make the lobster sauce, sweat the carrot, onion and
celery in the butter in a large heavy saucepan until softened. Chop the lobster heads and add to the pan. Cook
over moderately high heat about 10 minutes, stirring frequently. Add the Cognac and boil for a few seconds to
cook off the alcohol, then add the white wine and boil
until the liquid has reduced to a syrupy glaze. Add the
chopped tomato, tomato paste and garlic, continue cooking until most of the moisture from the tomato has evaporated, then add the fish stock or water, bouquet garni and
peppercorns and simmer uncovered for 1 hour, skimming
off any foam that rises to the surface. Remove from the
heat, let rest 10 minutes, then strain through a fine-
meshed strainer. There should be about 500ml/²⁄₃ pint/
2 cups of sauce.

To make the vinaigrette, combine the vinegar, mustard
and a little salt and pepper in a small bowl. Gradually
whisk in the oil until the vinaigrette has thickened and
emulsified. Cut the mushrooms into thin slices and toss
them with the lemon juice to prevent browning. Boil the
green beans, uncovered, in a pan of generously salted
water until just tender, 4-6 minutes, drain, and plunge

into ice water to stop the cooking and set their colour. Drain and reserve.

In a medium saucepan, simmer the strained lobster sauce until reduced to about 175ml/6fl oz/$^3/_4$ cup. Whisk in the butter a few pieces at a time to enrich the sauce and let cool slightly.

Reheat the lobster meat just until warm by simmering gently in the reserved cooking liquid. Slice the tail meat into medallions. Toss the salad greens, mushrooms and green beans with the vinaigrette and divide among 4 large plates. Drain the lobster meat and arrange it on top, recreating the form of the lobster and decorating with the tail fans. Drizzle a little warm lobster sauce over the lobster and the salad. Serve at once.

Note: The addition of the lobster sauce gives this salad an intriguing complexity of flavours, but a quicker alternative would be to omit the sauce and add to the vinaigrette one large tomato, peeled, seeded and diced, with 1 tbsp of chopped fresh herbs.

Traditional Burgundy Beef Stew

Boeuf bourguignon traditionnel au vin d'Irancy

SERVES 6

1kg/2lbs lean stewing beef or chuck, cut
in 2-inch pieces
6 tbsp plain (all-purpose) flour
salt and pepper
1 tbsp oil
3 tbsp butter
375ml/12fl oz/1½ cups beef or veal stock
3 slices bacon, cut in matchstick strips
½lb pearl onions, blanched and peeled
½lb button mushrooms, washed and
stems removed
hot cooked noodles, for serving

FOR THE MARINADE
1 onion, finely chopped
1 carrot, finely chopped
2 garlic cloves, finely chopped
1 bay leaf
½ tsp freshly ground pepper
2 cloves
750ml/1¼ pints/3 cups red wine (Irancy,
or other robust red burgundy wine)

Trim any fat from the meat. For the marinade, put the
chopped onion, carrot, garlic, bay leaf, pepper and cloves
into a large food storage bag. Put the bag in a large bowl,
add the meat, and pour over the wine. Seal the bag and

15

allow to marinate in the refrigerator for 24-48 hours, turning occasionally. Remove the meat from the marinade and blot dry on paper towels. Dredge in seasoned flour, a few pieces at a time.

Heat the oil and 1 tbsp of the butter in a heavy cast-iron casserole. Add the beef in one layer, not crowding the pan, and brown on all sides. Cook in batches, if necessary, and return the meat to the casserole when all is browned.

In a large saucepan, bring the marinade liquid and vegetables to a full boil, and skim off any foam that rises to the top. Pour over the meat in the casserole, and add the stock. Bring to a boil. Cover the casserole and simmer in a preheated 150°C / 300°F / gas mark 2 oven for 2 hours, or until very tender.

Meanwhile, cook the bacon until crisp, remove with a slotted spoon and drain on paper towels. In the same pan, brown the onions over moderate heat until evenly coloured. Remove with a slotted spoon, and reserve. Discard the bacon fat. Melt the remaining 2 tbsp of butter, and sauté the mushrooms until evenly browned.

After the stew has cooked about 1 hour, add the bacon, onions, and mushrooms to the casserole, and continue cooking for another hour.

Serve the beef stew from the casserole or in a heated serving dish, accompanied by cooked noodles.

Notes: The recipe can be doubled to serve 12, if wished. If preparing ahead, decrease cooking time by about 20 minutes. Reheat for about 45 minutes in a preheated 165°C / 325°F / gas mark 4 oven.

ASPARAGUS WITH TRUFFLE BUTTER

Asperges vertes au beurre de truffe

SERVES 4-6

750g/1¹/₂lb medium asparagus
1 tbsp finely chopped shallot
2 tbsp port wine
100ml/3¹/₂fl oz/7 tbsp truffle juice
125g/4oz/8 tbsp cold butter, cut in pieces
salt and pepper
15g/¹/₂oz fresh or preserved truffle, finely
chopped (optional)

Trim the ends from the asparagus. Peel the lower 2-3 inches, or the whole stem, if preferred. Tie the asparagus in 4-6 neat bundles for easier serving and to keep their shape during cooking. Cook the asparagus in boiling salted water or in a steamer until just tender.

Meanwhile, make the butter sauce. Put the shallot and port wine in a small heavy saucepan and boil until the wine has evaporated. Add the truffle juice, bring back to a boil and whisk in the butter over a high heat, 1 piece at a time. Remove from the heat and season to taste with salt and pepper.

To serve, reheat the sauce and add the chopped truffle, if using. Divide the asparagus among warm plates and remove the string. Pour a little of the sauce over the tips of the asparagus and pass the remainder.

TRIPLE-TIERED CHOCOLATE MOUSSE

Gâteau au chocolat noir

SERVES 6-8

400g/14oz good quality plain (semisweet)
chocolate, roughly chopped
2 eggs, separated
250ml/8fl oz/1 cup crème fraîche or
whipping cream
180g/6oz cake covering chocolate (also
called compound or confectioners'
chocolate)

To make the mousse, gently melt 200g/7oz of the plain (semisweet) chocolate in the top of a double boiler or using a microwave oven. Cool for a few minutes, then stir in the egg yolks. The mixture will thicken at this point, but keep stirring until it is smoother. Whip the egg whites until they form soft peaks. Stir about ¹/₃ of the egg whites into the chocolate mixture to lighten it, then carefully fold in the remaining whites, trying to maintain as much volume as possible. Whip the cream and carefully fold it into the chocolate mixture. Cover the mousse and refrigerate at least 2 and up to 24 hours.

For the chocolate tiers, combine the remaining 200g/7oz plain (semisweet) chocolate and the cake covering (compound) chocolate and melt gently in the top of a double boiler or using a microwave oven. Stir to mix the two chocolates completely. Line 2 or 3 baking sheets (be sure they are very flat) with parchment or waxed paper and set

3 tart rings 20cm/8 inches in diameter on top. Pour in the melted chocolate and spread into a smooth even layer with a rubber spatula or palette knife. (If you don't have tart rings, draw 3 circles on the parchment and spread the chocolate to an even round within. When the chocolate has almost set, trim the rounds to a perfect circle using a sharp knife.) Refrigerate the chocolate disks until solid, about 30 minutes.

When ready to assemble the dessert, run the tip of a knife around the inside of each ring, and carefully peel the chocolate disks from the paper. Place one on a round serving platter. Spread half of the mousse in an even layer over the surface of the disk. Alternatively, pipe the mousse in decorative rosettes using a large star tip. Place a second disk on top and add the remaining mousse. Top with the third disk (choose the most attractive one for the top). Keep the assembled dessert refrigerated until 30 minutes before serving.

Notes: The dessert can be tricky to cut, so you may want to present it whole to your guests, then return to the kitchen to dismantle the tiers, cut them and divide among the plates. The dessert could also be made in individual portions, using approximately 7.5cm / 3 inch circles. For a touch of colour, serve this dessert with a raspberry coulis, or the rich satiny mousse would be superb served on its own.

If cake covering (compound) chocolate is unavailable, you will need 600g / 1½lb plain (semisweet) chocolate: 200g / 7oz for the mousse and 400g / 14oz for the chocolate disks.

The Yonne, bending gracefully, link after link, through a never-ending rustle of poplar-trees, beneath lowly, vine-clad hills, with relics of delicate woodland here and there, sometimes close at hand, sometimes leaving an interval of broad meadow, has all the lightsome characteristics of French river-side scenery on a smaller scale than usual, and might pass for the child's fancy of a river, like the rivers of the old miniature-painters, blue, and full to a fair green margin.

WALTER PATER, *Imaginary Portraits*

FROGS' LEGS WITH BROAD (FAVA) BEANS AND MOREL MUSHROOMS

Cassolette de grenouilles, fèves vertes et morilles

SERVES 4

450g / 1lb frogs' legs
350g / 12oz fresh morel mushrooms
1kg / 2¼lbs fresh broad (fava) beans
60g / 2oz/4 tbsp butter
salt and pepper
250ml / 8fl oz/1 cup strong chicken stock
3-4 tbsp plain (all-purpose) flour
1 tbsp finely chopped shallot

Bone the frogs' legs with a small sharp knife. Set the meat aside. Trim and discard any tough or dirty ends from the morels and wash them in several changes of cool water until completely free of grit. Pat them dry on paper towels and cut any large ones into pieces. Set aside.

Shell the broad (fava) beans and cook them in boiling salted water until tender, about 15 minutes. Drain, then remove the skins by slitting the skin and gently squeezing out the bean. Toss with 1 tbsp of the butter and keep warm.

Meanwhile, in a frying pan, heat 2 tbsp of the butter over a moderately high heat and sauté the morels until they have rendered their liquid and are beginning to brown, about 5 minutes. Season with salt and pepper, add the chicken stock, reduce the heat and simmer gently another 8-10 minutes, until the morels are very tender and the liquid is reduced and concentrated in flavour. Remove from the heat and keep warm.

Just before serving, season the frogs' legs with salt and pepper and dredge them in the flour. Heat the remaining butter until foamy in a sauté pan, add the frog legs and the chopped shallot and sauté gently 1-2 minutes on each side, until golden brown.

To serve, remove the morels from their liquid with a slotted spoon and divide them among 4 shallow bowls or soup plates, mounding them in the centre. Arrange the frogs' legs and broad (fava) beans around the morels. Spoon over the morel cooking juices.

Notes: If the frogs' legs are not boned, increase cooking time to 3-5 minutes per side, or until springy to touch. Boneless chicken breast or veal tenderloin may be substituted for the frogs' legs. Dried morels (45g / 1^{1}/₂oz) may be used if fresh are not available. Soak them in hot water to cover for 20 minutes. Remove, rinse thoroughly, drain, then proceed with the recipe. The soaking liquid may be strained through a coffee filter to remove the grit and mixed with the chicken stock.

SHEPHERD'S PIE WITH EPOISSE CHEESE AND GARLIC SAUCE

*Le parmentier d'agneau au fromage d'Epoisse
sauce à l'ail*

SERVES 4

1kg/2¼lb boneless saddle of lamb
salt and pepper
1-2 tbsp olive oil
500g/1lb 2oz potatoes, peeled and cut
into large chunks
125ml/4fl oz/½ cup single (light) cream
or milk
125g/4oz ripe Epoisse cheese, cut into
small pieces
1 tbsp butter
2 garlic cloves, peeled and crushed
250ml/8fl oz/1 cup lamb or chicken
stock, or water
4 sprigs fresh thyme, for garnishing

With a sharp knife, trim the saddle of lamb to separate
the 2 loin pieces and the 2 smaller tenderloin pieces.
Trim the meatiest parts of the remaining flap sections,
and discard the fat and sinew. Season the tenderloins and
the flap trimmings with salt and pepper. In a heavy frying

pan, heat the oil and sauté the meat over a moderately high heat 4-5 minutes, until no longer pink. Set the meat aside to cool. Pour off the grease from the pan and reserve the pan for cooking the loin. The caramelized cooking juices in the pan will flavour the sauce. When the meat is cool, chop or grind it to make a 'hash'. Adjust seasoning.

Boil the potatoes in a pan of generously salted water for 15-20 minutes, until completely tender. Drain them, return to the pan, then mash them. Add the cream or milk and beat with a wooden spoon or a whisk to make a smooth purée. Add the cheese and butter, and beat again until the cheese is melted, then season to taste with salt and plenty of pepper.

Lightly butter a 20cm/8 inch square baking dish. Spread half the potato purée in an even layer. Arrange

the lamb hash on top, then top with the remaining potato mixture. Keep warm.

Season the lamb loins with salt and pepper. Heat a little more oil in the reserved sauté pan and sauté the loin pieces over moderately high heat until done to the desired degree, 8-10 minutes for medium-rare. Take care not to let the juices burn in the pan during cooking. Transfer the meat to a plate, cover it with foil and keep warm. Pour off any excess grease from the pan, then add the crushed garlic cloves and the stock or water. Boil, scraping to dissolve the caramelized juices, until the liquid has reduced to a few spoonfuls of concentrated sauce. Season with salt and pepper, if necessary, and strain.

Reheat the potatoes under a preheated grill (broiler) for 2-3 minutes, or until a golden crust forms. Cut the lamb loins into very thin slices, and pour any accumulated juices into the sauce. Put a few spoonfuls of the potato mixture in the centre of 4 warm plates and arrange the sliced loin around the edge. Spoon over a little sauce and top with a thyme sprig.

Notes: Epoisse cheese is a pungent cow's milk cheese whose rind is washed with Marc de Bourgogne during aging, giving it a distinctive tang and rusty colour. Other cheeses would be suitable for this dish, including Brie or Fontina. The potato dish may be prepared one day ahead, refrigerated, and reheated in a 190°C / 375°F / gas mark 6 oven for 30-35 minutes. Other cuts of lamb could be used, such as shoulder for the hash and neck fillet or even loin chops instead of sliced loin.

Seasonal Vegetables with Wild Mushroom Mousseline Sauce

L'assiette de légumes à la mousseline de champignons des bois

SERVES 6

100g / 3^{1}/$_{3}$oz wild mushrooms, such as
chanterelles or boletus mushrooms
1 tbsp vegetable oil
salt and pepper
750g / 1^{1}/$_{2}$lbs mixed seasonal vegetables,
washed and trimmed (green beans,
baby carrots, broccoli, cauliflower,
baby squash, etc)
1 tsp lemon juice
3 egg yolks
125g / 4oz / 8 tbsp unsalted butter, melted
125ml / 4fl oz / ^{1}/$_{2}$ cup crème fraîche or
whipping cream

Scrape the stems of the wild mushrooms to remove any soil or sand, and wipe the caps well with a damp cloth. Trim off the bottom stems if they are tough. Chop them coarsely and sauté in the oil over moderately high heat 4-6 minutes, until all their moisture has been rendered and they are golden brown. Season with salt and pepper, let cool slightly, then mince finely with a knife or in a food processor. Set aside.

Cook the vegetables in separate pans of boiling salted water or using a steamer until tender when pierced with a knife. Drain and keep warm.

To make the sauce, combine the lemon juice and egg yolks in the top of a double boiler and whisk, off the heat, until frothy. Place over very hot, but not boiling, water and continue to whisk rapidly until the egg yolks are thick and moussey and have at least doubled in volume. Remove from the heat and immediately whisk in the melted butter, a little at a time, to form a creamy emulsified sauce. Whip the crème fraîche or cream until it forms soft peaks, then gently fold it into the sauce with the chopped mushrooms. Season to taste with salt and pepper.

To serve, reheat the vegetables, if necessary, in a steamer or in a covered saucepan with a 2-3 tbsp boiling water in the bottom. Divide the mousseline sauce evenly among 6 warm plates and arrange the hot vegetables in a decorative pattern on top. Serve immediately.

APPLE AND BLACKCURRANT PARCELS WITH CINNAMON

La papillote de pommes et cassis à la cannelle

SERVES 4

4 medium apples (Cox's Orange Pippin,
Granny Smith, Golden Delicious)
1 tbsp lemon juice (optional)
2-4 tsp caster (superfine) sugar
1 tsp ground cinnamon
1 tbsp soft butter
175g / 6oz blackcurrants, removed from
the stem
4 tbsp crème de cassis
500ml / 16fl oz / 2 cups vanilla or cinnamon ice cream,
for serving (see page 69)

Preheat the oven to 200°C/400°F/gas mark 6. Peel the apples, cut into quarters, core and cut into thin slices. If not using immediately, toss with the lemon juice.

Combine the sugar and cinnamon in a small bowl, using the larger amount of sugar with tart apples.

Lightly butter 4 pieces of foil. Divide the blackcurrants among them, then arrange the apple slices on top. Pour 1 tbsp crème de cassis over each parcel and sprinkle each with one quarter of the cinnamon sugar. Fold up the edges and seal tightly.

Put the parcels on a baking tray and bake for 20 minutes.

To serve, put the parcels on individual plates. Slit open the parcels and top with a scoop of ice cream.

The road slanted down one of the side defiles, then turned at an angle, and I saw Avallon up against the sky, with the two convents and the church silhouetted, and the ring of wall still complete on this side. Up to the wall was carried an intricate work of terracing with steep paths between gardens, and in every garden the citizens of Avallon – most of whom are small *rentiers*, retired captains and the like – were pricking out their lettuces. At the bottom was the river, harnessed to drive the plant of half a dozen factories, tanning works, with great stacks of oak saplings piled in them. Up the valley, where the road got finally clear of houses, the gorge turned, and steep above me ran a great cliff of mingled wooding, lit with the flames of spring; and through the green and silver-grey and olive were many cherry-trees in blossom, shell-white and diaphanous, most aerial of all flowering things. Broom was bright too on the slopes, and I walked along in a maze of beauty and strangeness; for the gorge narrowed still closer, crags of granite stood out fantastically from the trees, giant rocks were tumbled in heaps: a Salvator Rosa country in the very heart of France.

STEPHEN GWYNN, *Burgundy* 1930

Burgundy in the summer is a corner of paradise. Warm and tranquil, the region quietly unveils its charms. There are thousands of hectares of woods, meadows, vineyards, rivers and lakes to whet the appetite. Fresh vegetables and fruit are in abundance; so too are farm chickens and the new season's lambs. Culinary dishes possess more imagination and diversity, incorporating a multitude of fresh ingredients and flavours. Yet the cuisine always remains true to the quality and authenticity of the products of the countryside. Meat may be fried and then enhanced with a sauce made of a local Burgundian wine, perhaps a young Irancy or something more typical such as Pommard; duck breast is cooked with a blackcurrant sauce; the whole gastronomy of the region adapts itself to the whims of the season with an astonishing serenity.

Radiant under the high rays of the sun, Nature is insatiable. It is impossible to end the gastronomic journey through the Burgundian summer without tasting one of the magnificent cow's milk cheeses for which the region is famous. A visitor to the area is seduced by the delights of cheeses such as Epoisse, Soumaintrain, Saint Florentin and Aisy Cendré.

M E N U S

Gazpacho with Dublin Bay Prawns and
Courgette (Zucchini) Mousse
*Gaspacho de langoustines à la crème
de courgettes*

Duck Breast with Blackcurrant Sauce
Aiguillettes de caneton sauce cassis

Braised Young Green Cabbage
Jeune choux vert braisé

Light Custard Cream with
Caramelized Pears
Crème chibouste aux poires caramélisées

Marinated Baby Vegetables
and Shellfish
*Grecque de légumes nouveaux et
coquillages*

Chicken Steamed in Red Wine
*La poularde fermière à la vapeur
de bourgogne*

Celeriac (Celery Root) Purée
with Nutmeg
Purée de celeriac à la muscade

Blackcurrant Bavarian Cream
Bavarois de cassis

S
U
M
M
E
R

GAZPACHO WITH DUBLIN BAY PRAWNS AND COURGETTE (ZUCCHINI) MOUSSE

Gazpacho de langoustines à la crème de courgettes

SERVES 4

300g / 10oz very small courgettes
(zucchini), trimmed and sliced
80ml / 2^1/$_2$fl oz / ^{1}/$_3$ cup whipping cream
^{1}/$_2$ tsp powdered gelatine (unflavored
gelatin), or 1 sheet gelatine (2g)
salt and pepper
20 Dublin Bay prawns or jumbo shrimp,
peeled
2 tsp olive oil

FOR THE GAZPACHO

750g / 1^1/$_2$lb ripe tomatoes, peeled, seeded
and chopped
7.5cm / 3 inch piece cucumber, peeled,
seeded and chopped
^{1}/$_2$ red (bell) pepper, cored and seeded
^{1}/$_2$ garlic clove, finely minced
4 spring onions (scallions), tough greens
removed
60g / 2oz white bread (about 2 slices),
crusts removed, torn into pieces
^{2}/$_3$ cup fresh tomato juice
1^1/$_2$ tsp olive oil
wine vinegar
salt and pepper

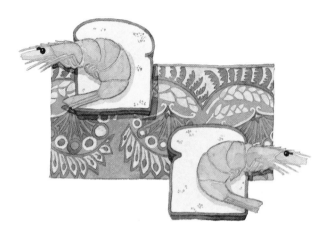

To make the gazpacho, purée the vegetables in a food processor. Soak the bread in the tomato juice and add to the puréed vegetables with the olive oil. Process to blend well. (Alternatively, put all the vegetables unpeeled in a juice extractor and use according to manufacturer's instructions. Pour the resulting juice over the bread and soak for 10 minutes, then purée with a hand blender.) Thin with as much of the tomato juice as needed. Season the gazpacho to taste with a few drops of wine vinegar, and salt and pepper. Strain, if wished, and refrigerate until ready to serve.

To make the courgette (zucchini) mousse, cook the courgettes in a large quantity of boiling salted water until very soft. Drain and purée in a food mill, or use a hand blender or food processor and strain afterwards. Put the purée in a heatproof bowl and pour 1 tbsp of the cream over the top. Sprinkle the gelatine over the surface and allow to stand 2-3 minutes until softened. (Alternatively, if using sheet gelatine, soak in cold water until soft, squeeze out excess water and add to the purée.) Put the bowl in a shallow pan of hot water over moderate heat and stir until the gelatine has dissolved and the purée is steaming. Let it cool, chill it, and when it begins to set, whip the remaining cream until it forms soft peaks. Beat in the courgette and gelatine mixture, season to taste with salt and pepper, and refrigerate at least $\frac{1}{2}$ hour, or until ready to serve.

When ready to serve, sauté the prawns in the olive oil over moderately high heat, turning once. When lightly coloured, remove and drain on kitchen paper (paper towels).

To serve, divide the gazpacho among 4 chilled soup plates. Using 2 teaspoons, scoop the mousse into small ovals and arrange 5 around the edge of the gazpacho in each soup plate. Place the prawns between the mounds of mousse, dividing them evenly, and serve immediately.

Notes: For a less complicated mousse, omit the courgettes (zucchini) and flavour the cream with herbs. Increase the amount of cream to 125ml/4fl oz/$\frac{1}{2}$ cup. Soften the gelatine in 3 tbsp of the cream in a small ramekin. Set the ramekin in a shallow pan of hot water over moderate heat and stir until the gelatin has dissolved. Let it cool, and when it begins to set, whip the remaining cream to soft peaks and beat in the gelatine mixture with 3 tbsp finely chopped fresh herbs, such as chives, parsley and basil or tarragon. Refrigerate to set.

If Dublin Bay prawns are not available, use other large prawns (jumbo shrimp).

DUCK BREAST WITH BLACKCURRANT SAUCE

Aiguillettes de caneton sauce cassis

SERVES 4

2 ducks, about 2.2kg / 5lb each
1 carrot, peeled and chopped
1 celery stick, chopped
1 small onion, peeled and chopped
200g / 7oz blackcurrants
125ml / 4fl oz / ½ cup red burgundy wine
1 garlic clove, peeled and crushed
bouquet garni (thyme sprigs, parsley
stems, bay leaf)
45g / 1½oz / 3 tbsp unsalted butter
2 dessert apples
1 tbsp duck fat
salt and pepper

Cut off the wings and the leg sections, and reserve the leg pieces for another use. Carefully cut down each side of the breastbone to remove the breasts. Pull off the skin, if you can, or cut the meat away from the skin if it adheres tightly. Wrap and refrigerate until needed.

Use the carcase and wings to make the stock for the sauce. Chop the duck carcase into several pieces. Melt a little of the fat from the duck in a heavy saucepan. Brown the wings with the carcase, turning from time to time. When well coloured, add the chopped vegetables. Cook 5 minutes longer, stirring occasionally. Pour off the accumulated fat and add the blackcurrants, with the wine. Boil until half of the wine has evaporated, then add water to cover and the garlic and bouquet garni. Bring to a boil, and skim off any foam that rises to the surface. Reduce the heat and simmer, partly covered, for 1 hour. Add a little more water if the ingredients are not mostly submerged. Strain the stock and remove the fat.

Melt 15g/1 tbsp of the butter in a nonstick frying pan and sauté the apples until golden brown, turning regularly. Keep warm.

Season the duck breasts on both sides. Heat the duck fat in a heavy frying pan and cook the duck breasts over moderately high heat for 1½-2 minutes per side. The meat should be pink and feel springy when pressed. Remove the duck breasts and keep warm while making the sauce. Pour off the fat and add the duck and blackcurrant stock to the pan. Boil until reduced to about 250ml/8fl oz/1 cup. Taste and adjust the seasoning, if necessary. Whisk in the remaining butter.

To serve, slice the duck breasts and arrange on each of 4 warm plates. Garnish with the apples. Pour some of the sauce over each serving and pass the remainder.

Notes: If blackcurrants are not available, raspberries make a good alternative. Redcurrants may be used, but they are less sweet; Crème de Cassis (blackcurrant liqueur) may be added to sweeten the sauce.

Braised Young Green Cabbage
Jeune choux vert braisé

SERVES 4

2 young green cabbages, about 1.5kg/3lb
60g/2oz streaky bacon (about 2 slices)
30g/1oz/2 tbsp butter
1 carrot, peeled and finely diced
1 small onion, peeled and finely chopped
bouquet garni (parsley stems, thyme
sprigs, bay leaf)
500ml/16fl oz/2 cups chicken stock or water
salt and pepper

Discard any damaged outer leaves from the cabbages and cut them in quarters. Remove the hard cores. Blanch them for 2 minutes in boiling salted water with 2 tbsp of vinegar. Refresh in cold water and drain well.

Cut the bacon in thin matchsticks. Melt half of the butter in a large cast iron casserole and add the bacon with the carrot and onion. Cover and cook over a moderate heat for 2 minutes. Add the cabbage, bouquet garni and stock. Transfer to a preheated 180°C/350°F/gas mark 4 oven and cook for 45 minutes, stirring occasionally. Season to taste. The cabbage can be prepared ahead and kept in its cooking liquid.

When almost ready to serve, gently boil the cabbage, uncovered, to evaporate the cooking liquid. Add the remaining tablespoon of butter, and taste and correct the seasoning, if necessary, before serving.

LIGHT CUSTARD CREAM WITH CARAMELIZED PEARS

Crème chibouste aux poires caramélisées

SERVES 4

2 firm ripe pears, about 180g/6oz each
1 tbsp unsalted butter
2 tbsp granulated sugar
3 eggs, separated
3 tbsp plain (all-purpose) flour
250ml/8fl oz/1 cup milk

FOR THE SYRUP
100g/3$\frac{1}{2}$oz/$\frac{1}{2}$ cup caster (superfine) sugar
60ml/2fl oz/$\frac{1}{4}$ cup milk

FOR THE SAUCE
200g/7oz/1 cup caster (superfine) sugar
125ml/4fl oz/$\frac{1}{2}$ cup water
125ml/4fl oz/$\frac{1}{2}$ cup whipping cream

Peel the pears, cut them in half, and remove the cores and stems. Cut the pears into 1cm/$\frac{3}{8}$ inch dice. Heat the butter in a small frying pan until foaming, and add the diced pears and 1 tbsp of the granulated sugar. Cook over a moderately high heat for 3-4 minutes, stirring or shaking the pan frequently, until the diced pears are lightly caramelized. Set aside to cool.

To make the custard cream, put the egg yolks and the remaining 1 tbsp granulated sugar in a medium-size mixing bowl and whisk until slightly thickened. Whisk in the flour until smooth. Bring the milk to a boil and pour a little of the boiling milk into the egg yolks, whisking constantly to avoid forming lumps of cooked egg. Gradually whisk in the remaining milk, then pour it all back into the saucepan. Cook over moderate heat for 4-5 minutes, whisking constantly, until the mixture is smooth and thick and has come back to a boil. Remove from the heat and stir in the vanilla essence (extract). Transfer to a mixing bowl and set aside to cool.

Combine the ingredients for the sugar syrup in a copper sugar pan or small heavy saucepan and cook over moderately high heat. Do not stir, but swirl the pan from time to time initially to help dissolve the sugar. Boil until the syrup reaches the hard-ball stage, 125°C/250°F. While the sugar is cooking, whip the egg whites until they form soft peaks. (Try to coordinate this so the egg whites and sugar syrup are ready at the same time. When the surface of the sugar mixture is covered with large bubbles, it is almost ready.) Slowly pour the sugar syrup into the egg whites in a thin stream, whisking constantly. The mixture will become thick and glossy. Continue whisking until the meringue is cool.

Stir a little of the meringue into the custard cream to lighten it, then carefully fold in the remaining meringue, trying to maintain as much volume as possible. Fold in all but about 4 tbsp of the caramelized pear. Lightly oil the inside of 4 tart rings 10cm/4 inches in diameter and set them on 4 dessert plates. Gently spoon the light custard cream into the rings and smooth the surface with the back of a spoon. Chill until ready to serve.

Meanwhile, make the caramel sauce. Put the caster (superfine) sugar and water in a copper sugar pan or small heavy saucepan and cook over a moderately high heat, swirling the pan from time to time initially to help dissolve the sugar. Boil until the sugar syrup is a deep amber colour. Remove from the heat and, holding the pan well away from you, add the cream. Stir until smooth.

To serve, gently lift off the tart rings and spoon some of the caramel sauce around the base of the desserts. Decorate the tops with the reserved caramelized pear and serve immediately.

Notes: If tart rings are unavailable, make rings of several layers of foil folded over several layers thick and secured with tape on the outside.

To test the sugar syrup without a thermometer, drop a small spoonful of the syrup into a glass of ice water, take the syrup and try to shape it between your fingers – when it is at the hard ball stage, it will form a firm, but pliable ball.

A veritable country of the vine, it presents never-theless an expression peaceful rather than radi-ant. Perfect type of that happy mean between northern earnestness and the luxury of the south, for which we prize midland France, its physiog-nomy is not quite happy – attractive in part for its melancholy. Its most characteristic atmos-phere is to be seen when the tide of light and dis-tant cloud is travelling quickly over it, when rain is not far off, and every touch of art or of time on its old building is defined in clear grey. A fine summer ripens its grapes into a valuable wine; but in spite of that it seems always longing for a larger and more continuous allowance of the sun-shine which is so much to its taste. You might fancy something querulous or plaintive in that rustling movement of the vine-leaves, as blue-frocked Jacques Bonhomme finishes his day's labour among them.

WALTER PATER, *Imaginary Portraits*

MARINATED BABY VEGETABLES AND SHELLFISH

Grecque de légumes nouveaux et coquillages

SERVES 4

1 litre / 1¼lb mixed clams and cockles
1 litre / 1¼lb mussels
2 artichokes
½ lemon
375ml / 12fl oz / 1½ cups white wine
375ml / 12fl oz / 1½ cups olive oil
375ml / 12fl oz / 1½ cups water
180ml / 6fl oz / ¾ cup lemon juice
1 tsp salt, or more to taste
½ tsp whole coriander seeds
½ tsp black peppercorns
1 clove
8 pickling (pearl) onions, peeled
8 small new carrots, green tops trimmed
½ small head cauliflower, trimmed into florets
125g / 4oz small button mushrooms, stems trimmed
1 courgette (zucchini), cut into
2.5 × 1cm / 1 × ⅜ inch sticks
3 ripe tomatoes, peeled, seeded and
diced
2 tbsp chopped fresh parsley

Soak the clams and cockles in cold water overnight.
Scrub the mussels under cold running water, and discard
any that are not firmly closed, or do not close when
tapped. Scrape off any loose barnacles and remove the
tuft of beard which may protrude from the edge of the
shells. Refrigerate until ready to use.

To prepare the artichokes, break off each stem close to the base. Starting from the bottom, pull off the first few layers of hard leaves, then cut the artichoke across about half way up and discard the leafy tops. Using a small stainless steel knife, trim the artichoke all around, starting from the stem, to remove all the green hard parts and expose the paler bottom and the fuzzy choke. Scrape out the choke with a spoon and discard. Rub the trimmed, cup-shaped artichoke bottoms with the lemon half as they are prepared to prevent discoloration.

To cook the vegetables, combine the white wine, olive oil, water, lemon juice, salt, coriander seeds, peppercorns, and clove in a large saucepan, and bring to a boil. Add the artichoke bottoms and simmer for 10 minutes, then add the remaining vegetables at 2 minute intervals in the following order: onions, carrots, cauliflower florets, mushrooms, courgettes (zucchini). Test the vegetables for tenderness. Finally, add the diced tomatoes and remove the vegetables from the heat. Do not drain. Cool to room temperature, cover and refrigerate.

To cook the shellfish, put the clams, cockles and mussels in a large pot and add about 125ml/4fl oz/$^1/_2$ cup of the vegetable cooking liquid. Cover, bring to a boil and cook over a high heat for about 5 minutes, shaking the pot frequently, until the shellfish open. Discard any that do not open after a few more minutes cooking. Drain the shellfish and reserve the cooking liquid. Strain it through a sieve lined with muslin (cheesecloth). Remove the shellfish from the shells and store in the strained cooking liquid, refrigerated, until needed.

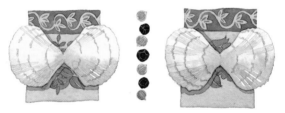

To assemble, drain the vegetables, reserve the liquid and put them into a chilled serving bowl. Remove the clams, cockles and mussels from their cooking liquid with a slotted spoon and add to the vegetables. Toss the vegetables and shellfish with a few tablespoons of both cooking liquids to moisten. Taste and adjust the seasoning. Sprinkle with chopped fresh parsley and serve with more reserved cooking liquid on the side, if wished.

CHICKEN STEAMED IN RED WINE

La poularde fermière à la vapeur de bourgogne

SERVES 4

1 free-range chicken, dressed weight
about 1.8kg / 3 ¹/₂lb, with giblets
salt and pepper
250g / ¹/₂lb plain (all-purpose) flour
60g / 2oz / 4 tbsp butter
extra chicken giblets (optional)
bouquet garni (parsley stems, thyme
sprigs, bay leaf)
625ml / 1 pint / 2 ¹/₂ cups homemade
chicken stock
500g / 1lb wild mushrooms, such as
boletus or oyster mushrooms

FOR THE MARINADE
1 bottle red burgundy wine
1 large carrot, peeled and finely chopped
(about ¹/₂ cup)
1 large onion, peeled and finely chopped
(about ²/₃ cup)

Remove giblets. Season the chicken inside and out with
salt and pepper. Put it in a glass or ceramic bowl just
large enough to contain it. Add the wine and chopped
vegetables, and allow to marinate for 3-4 hours at cool
room temperature or in the refrigerator.

Pour the marinating liquid into a large measuring container. Place an inverted ovenproof saucer or glass lid in
the bottom of a deep ceramic, earthenware or enamelled

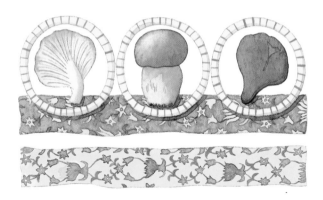

cast iron casserole to raise the bird above the liquid. Put the chicken on the saucer and reserve the marinade vegetables for the sauce. Add 375ml/12fl oz/1½ cups of the marinating liquid and cover the casserole. Make a paste to seal it by stirring cold water slowly into the flour to form a stiff dough. Roll the dough into a thin rope and press into the joint where the cover meets the casserole. Put the casserole into a preheated 190°C/375°F/gas mark 5 oven for 1½ hours.

Melt 1 tbsp of the butter in a large heavy saucepan, and brown the giblets until well coloured all over. Add the reserved marinade vegetables, bouquet garni, and the remaining marinating liquid. Boil until the liquid is almost all evaporated. Add the stock and boil gently to reduce by half. Remove the giblets and bouquet garni. Purée the sauce using a vegetable mill or food processor.

Scrape the stems of the mushrooms to remove any soil or grit, and wipe the caps well with a damp cloth. Trim off the bottom stems if they are tough. When almost ready to serve, melt the remaining butter in a large frying pan and sauté the mushrooms over moderately high heat. When they have rendered quite a bit of liquid, add the sauce. Reduce the heat and simmer gently until needed. Taste and adjust the seasoning, if necessary, before serving.

To serve, remove the flour paste seal and open the casserole at the table, so the aroma can be enjoyed by all. If preferred, return to the kitchen to carve the bird, or carve it at the table.

Notes: If the casserole has a tight-fitting lid, the flour paste seal is not absolutely necessary. The chicken may also be steamed in a pressure cooker (follow manufacturer's instructions). Make the sauce as above.

If chicken stock is not available use water, but never use stock made from bouillon cubes for a reduction sauce as it will become unpalatably salty.

CELERIAC (CELERY ROOT) PUREE WITH NUTMEG

Purée de celeriac à la muscade

SERVES 4

700g / 1½ lb celeriac (celery root)
1 litre / 1²/₃ pints / 4 cups milk or water
juice of ½ lemon (optional)
1 medium apple (150g / 5 oz), peeled
and quartered
1 medium potato (150g / 5 oz), peeled
and quartered
1 tbsp butter
4 tbsp whipping cream
½ tsp freshly grated nutmeg
salt and pepper

Peel the celeriac (celery root), cut into large pieces, and put into a large saucepan with the milk or water. If using water, add the lemon juice. Add the apple and potato, bring to a boil and cook gently until all are soft, 30-40 minutes. Drain well, and purée in a food processor or with a food mill or electric mixer. Add the butter, cream, and nutmeg and season to taste with salt and pepper. Return the purée to the saucepan to reheat very gently over a low heat. Serve hot with more nutmeg grated over the top.

BLACKCURRANT BAVARIAN CREAM
Bavarois de cassis

SERVES 4-6

450g / 1lb / 2½ cups blackcurrants
11g / 1 sachet / 2 scant tbsp powdered
gelatine (unflavored gelatin), or
6 gelatine sheets (2g each)
150ml / 5fl oz / ½ cup+2 tbsp milk
90g / 3oz / 6 tbsp granulated sugar
250ml / 8fl oz / 1 cup whipping cream

FOR THE SAUCE
225g / 8oz / 1¼ cups blackcurrants
150g / 5oz / ¾ cup granulated sugar, or
more to taste
180ml / 6fl oz / ¾ cup water

Purée the blackcurrants in a food processor or blender
and strain through a fine sieve. Alternatively work
through the fine mesh grill of a food mill. There should be
about 300ml / 10fl oz / 1¼ cups of blackcurrant purée.

If using powdered gelatine, put 2 tbsp of the milk in a
small bowl. Sprinkle the gelatine over the surface and
allow to stand 2-3 minutes until softened. Combine the
remaining milk and the sugar in a sucepan and bring to a
boil, stirring to dissolve the sugar. Reduce the heat to

low, add the softened gelatine, and stir until the gelatine has dissolved completely. Alternatively, if using sheet gelatine, soak in cold water until soft and squeeze out excess water before adding to the milk and sugar after it has come to a boil and the heat has been reduced. Let the mixture cool to room temperature. Combine with the blackcurrant purée in a large bowl and stir to mix thoroughly.

Place the bowl over a larger bowl filled with ice water, or set it in a baking dish filled with ice water. Stir with a rubber spatula, scraping down the sides frequently, until it is cold and slightly thickened.

In another bowl, whip the cream until it forms soft peaks. Stir about 1/3 of the whipped cream into the blackcurrant mixture to lighten it, then carefully fold in the remaining cream, trying to maintain as much volume as possible. Set a 20cm/8 inch diameter tart ring on a flat round serving plate and pour in the bavarian cream mixture. Alternatively, pour the mixture into a 20cm/8 inch diameter springform pan. Cover and chill at least 6 hours, or overnight.

To make the sauce, reserve a few of the blackcurrants for decoration and combine the rest with the sugar and water in a saucepan. Bring to a boil and simmer for 10 minutes, stirring occasionally. Taste and add more sugar if a sweeter sauce is desired. Strain the sauce through a fine sieve and chill until needed.

To serve, run a thin knife around the inside of the ring and gently lift it from the bavarian cream. If using a springform pan, remove the sides and set on a serving plate. Decorate with the reserved blackcurrants and serve, cut in slices, with the blackcurrant sauce.

Note: This is a light and refreshing dessert with a stunning magenta colour. For a simpler presentation, the bavarian mixture, once set, could be scooped into balls or ovals and served in bowls or coupé glasses, with a little of the sauce spooned on top.

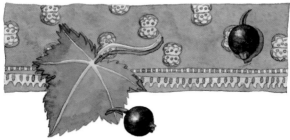

A U T U M N

Purists will tell you that anyone who has not seen Burgundy in autumn does not know anything of this ancient and peaceful region. In order to whet the appetite in these short yet still warm days, you have to open your eyes, prick up your ears and smell all the tormented perfumes of a world of greenery which is fading away. The senses have to be sharpened for savouring a cuisine which is more hearty, more rustic and more comfortable, with dishes that are full of character.

The glowing colours of autumn are perfect for this rustic cuisine which heralds a culinary contest with the long meals of winter. The dying summer shoots its last arrows with rare and flavourful delicacies – late-season melons and salads. Autumn's palette of tawny colours can be enjoyed in the delicious flavours and fragrances of the foods of the forest, and in the cooking juices of meats. It is the ideal season for sampling the great Burgundian wines at their peak, accompanying local products such as salt- and freshwater fish, pâtés and game. Hare, rabbit and pheasant appear on the menu, together with partridge roasted with a sauce of Marc de Bourgogne and local mushrooms, capturing the essence of this atmospheric late season.

MENUS

Scallops Wrapped in Celeriac
Les Saint Jacques poêlées en bardes de céleri au jus légèrement truffé

Partridge with Boletus Mushrooms
Perdreau rôti aux cèpes

Potato Cakes
Galette de pommes de terre olympique

Layered Apples with Apple Mousse and Quince Sauce
Croquant de pommes au jus de coing

Mussels with New Potatoes and Saffron Broth
Bouille de moules de bouchot et pommes de terre nouvelles au safran

Pigeon with Grapes and Marc de Bourgogne
Pigeon fermier aux raisins et au Marc de Bourgogne

Pears in Puff Pastry
Feuilleté aux poires caramélisées

Ginger Ice Cream
Glace gingembre

SCALLOPS WRAPPED IN CELERIAC
Les Saint Jacques poêlées en bardes de céleri au jus légèrement truffé

SERVES 4

1 medium celeriac (celery root)
1 tbsp vinegar or lemon juice
1 onion, peeled and finely chopped
1 large or 2 small carrots, peeled and
finely chopped
45g/1½oz lean smoked back bacon or
ham, finely chopped
salt and pepper
2-3 tbsp butter
20 sea scallops
2 tsp truffle juice
deep-fried celery leaves, for garnishing

Peel the celeriac and cut in half. Place one half cut side down on a board and trim off the sides to leave a piece about 2.5cm/1 inch wide. Turn the piece on its side and slice very thinly into ribbons no more than 1.5mm/¹⁄₁₆ inch thick. Repeat with the remaining half to obtain 20 thin slices long enough to go around the scallops. If the slices are not sufficiently long to wrap the scallops, 2 slices per scallop will be needed. Parboil the strips of celeriac in boiling salted water with the vinegar or lemon juice for 3-4 minutes, or until just tender. Drain on paper, blot well and allow to cool.

Cut the remaining celeriac into very small cubes. The quantity should be approximately equal to the amount of chopped onion and carrots. Put all the vegetables with the bacon or ham into a heavy saucepan. Season them lightly with salt and pepper, cover and sweat over a low heat until the vegetables are soft, stirring occasionally. Add a little butter, if necessary, to prevent them sticking. Keep warm off the heat until serving.

Drain and blot the scallops dry. Season them and wrap each with a strip of celeriac secured with a wooden pick. Use two strips if necessary, overlapping at the sides. Heat enough butter to coat the bottom of a frying pan which will hold the scallops in one layer. When the butter is foamy, add the scallops and cook over a moderately high heat for about 3 minutes per side, or until the celeriac is lightly browned and the scallops have rendered some liquid.

Divide the vegetable mixture among 4 warm plates, spreading it in a thin layer. Arrange 5 scallops on each plate. Add the truffle juice to the cooking liquid from the scallops, heat through and pour over each serving. Garnish with deep fried celery leaves and serve immediately.

Notes: If the scallops have not rendered some liquid from cooking, heat 3-4 tbsp of chicken stock in the pan in which the scallops were cooked to make the sauce.

Fresh celery leaves or flat-leaf parsley may be used for garnishing instead of deep-fried celery leaves.

Partridge with
Boletus Mushrooms

Perdreau rôti aux cèpes

SERVES 4

4 young partridges, dressed and drawn
salt and pepper
4-6 tbsp butter
4 large boletus mushrooms
300ml/½ pint/1¼ cups strong poultry or
game bird stock
4 potato cakes, for serving (see page 58)
watercress, for garnishing

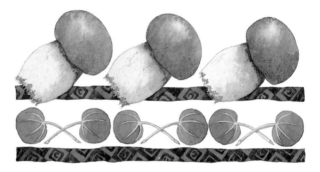

Preheat the oven to 230°C/450°F/gas mark 8.

Wipe the birds, season them inside and out with salt
and pepper and truss them. Melt 1 tbsp of the butter in a
heavy roasting pan or cast-iron casserole large enough to
contain the birds and lightly brown them on all sides.
Transfer the pan to the oven and roast the birds for 4 minutes on each leg. Remove from the oven and allow the
birds to rest for 10 minutes breast up.

Meanwhile, scrape the stems of the mushrooms to remove any soil or sand and wipe the caps well with a damp cloth. Trim off the bottom of the stems if necessary. Cut the mushrooms into slices about 1cm /³⁄₈ inch thick, with the cap attached to the stem.

When the partridges have rested, remove the leg quarters and pull the back away from the breast section, removing the wishbone and collar bones. As the birds are still hot, clean rubber gloves are useful to protect your hands. Detach the fillets from the breastbone, if wished, or leave the breast section whole for serving. Cover the partridge pieces and keep warm. Brown the carcases in 1 tbsp of butter in a heavy saucepan. Add the stock and boil to reduce by about half.

Melt 2 tbsp of butter in a large frying pan. Season the mushrooms and sauté them over a moderately high heat until browned.

Strain the sauce, and taste for seasoning. Whisk in 1-2 tbsp cold butter, if wished, for a richer sauce.

To serve, reheat the partridge pieces in the oven for 4-5 minutes with the potato cakes. Arrange one quarter of the mushroom slices on each of 4 warm plates with a potato cake on top. Place a breast crown or 2 fillets on each potato cake with the legs on either side of the breasts to resemble the whole bird. Garnish with watercress bouquets. Pour over a little of the sauce and serve the remainder on the side.

Potato Cakes
Galette de pommes de terre olympique

SERVES 4

3 potatoes, about 125g/4oz each
clarified butter, for frying
salt and pepper

Buy long, cylindrical potatoes, rather than round ones.
Peel them and trim as necessary to form even cylinders.
Using an apple corer, remove the centre. Slice the potatoes
crosswise into thin even slices no more than 1.5mm/
$^1/_{16}$ inch thick. A precision cutting tool such as a mandoline slicer is good for this, but a food processor will work,
although it may be difficult to control the cutting angle.

Brush a large heavy frying pan or griddle with enough
clarified butter to coat the bottom. Arrange the potato
rings overlapping in concentric circles to form lacy disks,
each approximately 15cm/6 inches in diameter. Season
lightly and cook over a moderate heat until golden brown.
Turn the potato cakes over very gently and press down
firmly to help the slices stick together. Cook until
browned on the other side. Serve immediately or set aside
on a warm plate until needed. The potato cakes may be
made up to 1 hour ahead and reheated in the frying pan
or on a baking sheet in a hot oven for a few minutes.

Notes: Unsalted butter and vegetable oil in equal proportions
may be used in place of clarified butter.

The potato cakes can be made from whole slices of potato
instead of rings if no apple corer is available.

LAYERED APPLES WITH APPLE MOUSSE AND QUINCE SAUCE

Croquant de pommes au jus de coing

SERVES 4

FOR THE DRIED APPLES
75g/6 tbsp granulated sugar
250ml/8fl oz/1 cup water
2 Golden Delicious apples

FOR THE FILLING
2 Golden Delicious apples
60g/5 tbsp caster (superfine) sugar
3 tbsp cold water
125ml/4fl oz/$^{1}/_{2}$ cup whipping cream, whipped
175g/6oz/$^{3}/_{4}$ cup cold apple purée (applesauce)
pinch ground cinnamon

FOR THE SAUCE
180g/6oz/$^{3}/_{4}$ cup quince jelly
1-2 tbsp lemon juice
mint leaves, for decorating

To make the dried apple slices, put the sugar and water in a saucepan and bring to a full boil, stirring as necessary to dissolve the sugar. Set the syrup aside to cool. Peel the apples, remove the core with an apple corer and

slice crossways about 5mm/¼ inch thick. Put the slices
into the syrup and macerate overnight. Remove the apple
slices from the syrup and drain them. Arrange them on a
lightly buttered baking sheet and put in a preheated
140°C/280°F/gas mark 1 oven until the slices are lightly
coloured and dried. Allow them to cool completely and
store in an airtight container.

To make the caramelized apples for the filling, peel
and core the apples and cut into 5mm/¼ inch dice. Put
the sugar in a copper sugar pan or small heavy saucepan
with 1 tbsp of the water. Do not stir, but swirl the pan
from time to time initially to help dissolve the sugar. Boil
over a high heat until it turns a light golden brown. Holding the pan well away from you, add the diced apple and
continue cooking until the apple is tender and nicely
coloured. Add the remaining 2 tbsps of water to stop the
cooking. Set aside to cool.

To make the sauce, melt the quince jelly over low heat
and thin with lemon juice to taste. Cool to room temperature.

To assemble the desserts, whip the cream and fold in
the apple purée with a little cinnamon. Drain the
caramelized apples if they are watery and gently fold
them into the mixture. Put a spoonful of this mousse on
each of 4 plates and lay one of the smallest apple slices
on each. Top with some more mousse and a larger apple
slice. Repeat the layering, selecting varying sized apple
slices to reconstruct the shape of the whole apples and
using a quarter of the filling mixture for each dessert.

Pour several spoonfuls of quince sauce around the base
of each 'apple' to serve, and decorate with a mint leaf.

Burgundy should not be visited when the vineyards are leafless and the cornfields bare, for it is essentially a land of corn and wine; and it is perhaps at the greatest height of its beauty at the end of June, when the standing crops are growing golden and are interspersed with patches of vines, thick with heavy green leaves. For the forest-lands and that part of the Côte d'Or which constitutes the actual wine-country, late September is the best. Then Nature shows more brilliant colours than at any other time of the year. Vineyards and woods glow red and yellow, and the horizon becomes a deeper blue. The days of rain may come, but they are succeeded by days of golden sunshine and an atmosphere clear as crystal, as if the air had been washed and had been left bright and shining. The sight of the great bunches of ripened grapes gives a feeling of expectancy, for in the first days of October the vintage will begin.

EVELYN M. HATCH,
Burgundy Past and Present 1927

MUSSELS WITH NEW POTATOES AND SAFFRON BROTH

Bouille de moules de bouchot et pommes de terre nouvelles au safran

SERVES 4

400g / 1lb cockles (or small clams)
1 litre / 1¼lb mussels
1 small carrot, peeled and finely chopped
1 celery stick, finely chopped
1 small leek (white part only), peeled and finely chopped
2 tbsp butter
4 small tomatoes, peeled, seeded and finely chopped
½ tsp saffron threads
400ml / 13fl oz / 1⅔ cups water
bouquet garni (leek greens, bay leaf and thyme sprigs, tied together)
salt and pepper
4 new potatoes, about 450g / 1lb total
1 egg yolk
1 small garlic clove, peeled
100ml / 6 tbsp olive oil
lemon juice
hot pepper sauce (optional)
2 shallots, peeled and chopped
100ml / 6 tbsp dry white wine

Soak the cockles in cold water overnight.

Scrub the mussels under cold running water, and discard any which are not firmly closed or which do not close when tapped. Scrape off any loose barnacles and remove the tuft of 'beard' which may protrude from the edge of the shells.

To make the broth, sweat the chopped carrots, celery and leek in half the butter for 1 minute. Add the chopped tomato and half the saffron, the water and bouquet garni.

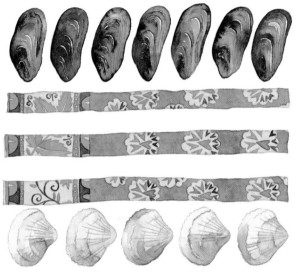

Season with a tiny pinch of salt and a little pepper and simmer over low heat, covered, for 20 minutes.

Cook the potatoes in their skins in boiling salted water and peel when they are cool enough to handle. Trim off the ends, reserving them for the garlic mayonnaise sauce.

Soften the remaining saffron in 1 tbsp of boiling water. Push the potato trimmings through a sieve into a small deep bowl. Add the egg yolk and the garlic, which has been pushed through a garlic press or very finely chopped. Beat the mixture with an electric mixer until smooth. Add the oil in a thin stream while beating constantly until it thickens like a stiff mayonnaise. Dilute the sauce with the saffron water. Season to taste with salt and pepper, a few drops of lemon juice and a dash hot pepper sauce, if using. Alternatively, make the sauce in a food processor or blender.

Put the cockles and mussels in a heavy saucepan or casserole with the shallots and wine. Cover and cook over a high heat for about 3 minutes, or until the mussels have opened. Strain the cooking liquid through a fine sieve lined with damp muslin. Remove the cockles and mussels from their shells.

To serve, slice the potatoes thinly and arrange them in a circle in heatproof soup plates. Put these in a low oven for about 5 minutes to reheat. Add the strained cooking liquid to the saffron vegetable broth and bring to a boil.

Heat the remaining butter in a frying pan over moderately high heat until foamy. Add the seafood and cook long enough to heat through.

Put a spoonful of the garlic mayonnaise in the centre of each soup plate and divide the cockles and mussels among them. Pour the hot broth over and serve immediately.

Note: For a simpler presentation of this dish, reheat the potato slices and shellfish in the broth and serve with a dollop of sauce on top. In this case, only half the given amount of butter will be needed.

PIGEON WITH GRAPES AND MARC DE BOURGOGNE

Pigeon fermier aux raisins et au Marc de Bourgogne

SERVES 4

4 squab pigeons, about 400g/14oz each
500ml/16fl oz/2 cups red wine
4 tbsp wine vinegar
3 tbsp chopped onion
3 tbsp chopped carrot
1 garlic clove, crushed
300g/10oz wild mushrooms (boletus or
oyster mushrooms, if possible)
40 red grapes
125ml/4fl oz/$\frac{1}{2}$ cup strong poultry or
game bird stock (optional)
salt and pepper
4 tbsp butter
4 tbsp Marc de Bourgogne
160ml/$\frac{1}{4}$ pint/$\frac{2}{3}$ cup whipping cream
1 tbsp chopped shallots
parsley sprigs

Put the pigeons in a glass or ceramic bowl just large enough to hold them. Pour over the red wine and wine vinegar and add the chopped onion and carrot, and the garlic. Leave them to marinate for 4 hours in a cool place.

Clean the mushrooms and cut in 1.5cm/$\frac{1}{2}$ inch dice, or slice them thinly. If the grapes are not seedless, carefully remove the seeds with the point of a knife.

About 45 minutes before serving, preheat the oven to

200°C/400°F/gas mark 6. Remove the pigeons from the marinade and start reducing it over a high heat, adding the stock if using. Skim off the foam from time to time and boil until it has reduced by half.

Wipe the pigeons dry and season them with salt and pepper. Melt 1 tbsp of the butter in a heavy cast-iron casserole and brown the birds over a moderate heat, turning them on all four sides until evenly browned. Remove from the heat, cover the casserole and continue cooking in the oven for 10-12 minutes, or until the juices run clear when the bird is pierced.

Remove the pigeons and keep warm. Deglaze the casserole with the Marc de Bourgogne. Flame it, then strain the reduced marinade mixture into the casserole and reduce by half. Add the cream and continue reducing until the sauce is smooth and syrupy. Add the grapes and cook for a few minutes. Taste the sauce and adjust the seasoning.

Meanwhile, melt the remaining butter and fry the mushrooms until golden, adding the shallots toward the end of the cooking.

To serve, arrange the pigeons on a warmed serving platter or on individual plates. Nap the pigeons with a little of the sauce, spooning out the grapes. Surround the birds with the sautéed mushrooms and garnish with sprigs of parsley. Pass the remaining sauce separately.

Notes: Wood pigeons are generally smaller and are usually served pink, so they will need less cooking time, about 8-10 minutes in the oven, or until the juices run slightly pink.

If Marc de Bourgogne is not available, substitute grape brandy or Cognac.

Pears in Puff Pastry

Feuilleté aux poires caramélisées

SERVES 6

150g/5oz/³/₄ cup granulated sugar
500ml/16fl oz/2 cups water
3 large pears, William or Bartlett
juice of 1 lemon
¹/₂ vanilla bean
450g/1lb puff pastry
600ml/1 pint/2¹/₂ cups ginger ice cream,
for serving (see page 69)
4 tbsp chopped roasted pistachios or
almonds
mint leaves, for decorating (optional)

FOR THE SAUCE
75g/2¹/₂oz/6 tbsp caster (superfine) sugar
125ml/4fl oz/¹/₂ cup water
2 large pears, peeled, cored and diced
1 tsp grated fresh ginger root

Put the sugar and water in a saucepan, and bring to a boil and remove from the heat. Peel and core the pears and put them into the syrup with the lemon juice and vanilla bean. Poach them over a moderate heat until just tender, about 10 minutes, or longer if the pears are not ripe. Cool the pears in the syrup and chill until needed.

Roll out the pastry into a rectangle about 3mm / ¹/₈ inch thick. Trim the sides to form a neat rectangular shape and cut it into 6 squares. Chill at least ¹/₂ hour and bake in a preheated 190°C / 375°F / gas mark 5 oven until puffed and well browned. Keep warm if not using immediately.

Meanwhile, make the sauce. Put the sugar in a copper sugar pan or small heavy saucepan with 2 tbsps of the water. Do not stir, but swirl the pan from time to time initially to help dissolve the sugar. Boil over a high heat until it turns a light golden brown. Holding the pan well away from you, add the remaining water to stop the cooking and dilute the caramel. Add the diced pear and cook over a moderate heat until they are tender. Add the ginger and leave to infuse for 5 minutes. Purée with a hand blender or in a food processor and strain the sauce.

To serve, split open the puff pastry squares with a serrated knife. Cut each pear half in thin slices the long way and fan the slices out on the bottoms of the pastry, draping them over the edges. Put the sauce between the slices, dividing it evenly among the servings. Using two large spoons, shape the ice cream into ovals and put two or three on each pastry bottom. Sprinkle each serving with a tbsp of chopped nuts. Lay the puff pastry tops at an angle partly covering the bottom half of the pastries and serve immediately, decorated with mint leaves, if using.

GINGER ICE CREAM

Glace gingembre

SERVES 4-6

250ml / 8fl oz / 1 cup milk
60g / 2oz / $^{1}/_{3}$ cup granulated sugar
15g / 1$^{1}/_{2}$ tsp grated fresh ginger root
3 egg yolks
125ml / 4fl oz / $^{1}/_{2}$ cup whipping cream

Bring the milk to a boil in a heavy saucepan with 1 tbsp of the sugar and the ginger. Remove from the heat just as it begins to bubble and let it infuse for a few minutes.

Beat the egg yolks with the remaining sugar until thick and pale, about 2 minutes. Strain the milk and whisk it into the egg yolk mixture. Pour it all back into the saucepan and cook over a moderate to low heat, stirring constantly, until the custard has thickened and will coat the back of a spoon, about 10 minutes. To test, remove the spoon and draw a line across the back with a finger: the line should remain and not begin to fill in. Transfer to another container and let stand, then chill until cold.

Add the cream to the cold custard and stir to combine well. Pour the mixture into an ice cream machine and freeze according to manufacturer's instructions.

Note: For vanilla ice cream, omit the ginger and infuse the milk with 1 vanilla pod, split lengthways and the inside scraped to release the seeds into the milk. For cinnamon ice cream, infuse the milk with 2 cinnamon sticks.

WINTER

Harsh and often cold, winter nevertheless retains a human face in a region where the seasons are clearly defined. Temperatures which in high summer exceed 35°C fall below 10°C in mid-winter. This is the season of short grey mornings, often misty in the northern parts of Burgundy along the banks of the river Yonne. The shorter the days, the longer the meals, which become hearty and gourmand. Culinary flights of fancy are put on hold dishes are carefully put together and more conventional. In winter the gourmet is bowled over by the simplicity and subtle harmony of flavours. Rich aromas float from the ovens and evoke the rustic simplicity of country dishes. Game products are at their best, in particular venison and wild boar. Dijon's famous mustard is used in many culinary preparations to warm the tastebuds, and the humble potato and onion regain their nobility. Red meat, poultry and rabbit dishes are accompanied by winter vegetables like cabbage and carrots. The chilled desserts of summer are forgotten as the cuisine focuses on traditional baking, crêpes and chocolate desserts which help to put aside all thoughts of the harshness of the weather and the days that are over too quickly.

M E N U S

Snails with Parsley Purée and
Tomato Sauce
*Escargots petits gris au persil et à la
fondue de tomate*

Stuffed Saddle of Rabbit with
Mustard Sauce
*Rable de lapereau à la moutarde
sauce tranchée*

Potato and Onion Gratin with Red Wine
*Gratin de pommes de terre et d'oignons
au vin rouge*

Bitter Chocolate Wafers with Almond
Praline Cream
*Fines feuilles de chocolat amer et crème
légère pralinée*

Calf's Liver with Poached Egg and
Red Wine Sauce
Foie de veau et oeuf de poule en meurette

Wild Duck with Brussels Sprouts
*Canard sauvage à l'embeurée de choux
de Bruxelles*

Carrot Flans
Petites timbales de carottes

Warm Candied Grapefruit Crêpes with
Grapefruit Sorbet
Petites crêpes et pamplemousse en chaud-froid

W
I
N
T
E
R

71

SNAILS WITH PARSLEY PUREE AND TOMATO SAUCE

Escargots petits gris au persil et à la fondue de tomate

SERVES 4

1kg/2lb ripe tomatoes
60g/2oz/4 tbsp butter
3 tbsp finely chopped shallots
bay leaf
salt and pepper
375g/³/₄ lb fresh curly-leaf parsley, washed
200-250ml/6-8fl oz/³/₄-1 cup crème fraîche or whipping cream
48 cooked snails, or 2 cans snails (115g/ 4oz drained weight), rinsed and drained well

To make the tomato sauce, core the tomatoes and immerse in boiling water for 1 minute. Drain, peel them, and cut in half through the 'equator'. Squeeze out the seeds and chop the flesh finely. Heat 1 tbsp of the butter in a saucepan and sweat 2 tbsp of the shallots until soft, about 2 minutes. Add the tomatoes and bay leaf and cook uncovered over a moderately low heat until the liquid has evaporated, about 30 minutes, stirring occasionally. Season to taste with salt and pepper. Remove the bay leaf.

Meanwhile, make the parsley purée. Remove the parsley leaves from the stems and put in a large measuring container: there should be 2 litres /3¹/₄ pints /8 cups loosely packed. Cook the parsley leaves in a large quantity of boiling salted water until it is tender, 3-4 minutes.

Drain and refresh in cold water to stop the cooking and set the colour. Squeeze out all the water by small handfuls. Purée using a food processor or in a food mill fitted with the fine grill. This process may be done ahead, if preferred. For serving, bring the minimum amount of cream to a boil in a small heavy saucepan, add the parsley purée and heat through, stirring constantly. Stir in 1½ tbsp of the butter and, if necessary, add the remaining cream a spoonful at a time to make the purée soft but not runny. Season to taste with salt and pepper and keep warm.

Melt the remaining 1½ tbsp of butter in a frying pan and add the remaining 1 tbsp chopped shallots with the snails. Cook for 2-3 minutes until the shallots have softened and the snails are hot. Season to taste with salt and pepper.

To serve, reheat the tomato sauce, if necessary. Put the snails in the centre of 4 warm plates, dividing them evenly. Spoon a quarter of the tomato sauce in a ring around the snails. Spoon a ring of parsley purée to surround it, dividing it evenly.

STUFFED SADDLE OF RABBIT WITH MUSTARD SAUCE

Rable de lapereau à la moutarde sauce tranchée

SERVES 4

2 rabbit saddles
2 rabbit forequarters or hindquarters
salt and pepper
4 tbsp white port or sherry
$^3/_4$ cup whipping cream
75g/2$^1/_2$oz/5 tbsp butter
2 heads butterhead (Boston) lettuce
60g/2oz/streaky bacon (about 2 slices)
$^1/_2$ tsp fresh thyme leaves, or $^1/_4$ tsp dried thyme
freshly grated nutmeg
125ml/4fl oz/$^1/_2$ cup dry white wine
250g/$^1/_2$lb chanterelle mushrooms
1$^1/_2$ tbsp Dijon mustard

FOR THE STOCK
rabbit bones
1 large carrot, finely chopped
1 large onion, finely chopped
1 large leek, finely chopped
1 litre/1$^2/_3$ pints/4 cups water
bouquet garni (parsley stems, thyme
sprigs, bay leaf)

Start preparing this dish 2 days before serving. Although time-consuming, much of the work can be done ahead. To bone the saddles, with a small knife, press along one side of the backbone to locate the rack of short bones, then cut along the underside of these bones to free the fillet, continuing down the carcase until the meat is separated from the bone. Do not remove the belly flap from the fillet, as it will enclose the stuffing. Remove the meat from the rabbit forequarters or hindquarters to use for the stuffing; there should be about 200g / 7oz boneless meat. Reserve the bones for the stock.

Season the saddles with salt and plenty of pepper. Sprinkle each with a tbsp of port or sherry, roll up and put in a small dish with the boneless stuffing meat. Pour on the cream, adding a little more, if necessary, to cover the meat. Cover the dish and marinate in the refrigerator for 48 hours.

To make the stock, melt 1 tbsp of the butter in a large heavy saucepan and sauté the rabbit bones over a moderately high heat. When the bones are browned, add the vegetables and continue cooking, stirring frequently, until the vegetables are coloured. Add the stock or water,

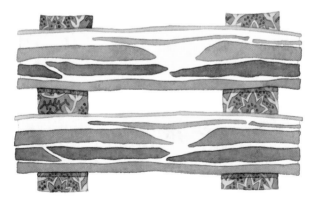

topping up with more liquid, if necessary, to cover the ingredients. Bring to a boil, add the bouquet garni, reduce the heat and simmer gently for 2 hours, partially covered, until the liquid is reduced by about one third. Strain the rabbit stock, chill and remove the fat.

The day of serving, prepare the lettuce. Remove any damaged leaves and blanch the heads, one at a time in a large pot of boiling salted water. Refresh in cold water and drain well. Cut out the cores, squeeze out all the water, and chop the leaves finely. Reserve 2 tablespoons of the chopped lettuce for the stuffing and refrigerate the rest until ready to serve.

Take the boneless saddles from the marinating cream and wipe off the cream. Remove the stuffing meat from the cream with a slotted spoon and transfer to a food processor or meat grinder. Mince it with the bacon, adding another 1-2 tbsp of the marinating cream if the mixture seems dry. Mix in the reserved cooked lettuce and season with thyme, nutmeg, plenty of pepper and a little salt. Unroll the saddles and put one quarter of the stuffing along the side of each fillet. Enclose the stuffing in the flap, rolling up to make a neat round cylinder. Tie each with string and refrigerate if not cooking immediately. Reserve the marinating cream for the sauce.

About $1\frac{1}{2}$ hours before serving, melt 1 tbsp of the butter in a heavy cast-iron casserole and brown the rabbit parcels on all sides. Add the wine and the stock. Bring to a boil, reduce the heat and simmer gently for 1 hour, or until the rabbit parcels are very tender. Remove the parcels and keep warm, covered. Boil the cooking liquid to reduce by two-thirds. Add the cream and continue boiling to reduce by half. Meanwhile, melt 1½ tbsp of the remaining butter in a heavy frying pan and sauté the mushrooms, stirring occasionally, until browned. Cook the chopped lettuce in the remaining 1½ tbsp butter over a moderately low heat to heat through.

Stir the mustard into the sauce; taste and adjust the seasoning, adding a little more mustard if wished. If necessary, reheat the rabbit parcels in the sauce.

To serve, slice the parcels and arrange overlapping slices on each of 4 warmed plates. Garnish with the mushrooms and cooked lettuce. Pour a little of the sauce over the meat and serve the remainder separately.

Note: If rabbit pieces are not available separately, use 1 rabbit about 1.8kg/4lb dressed weight. Use the saddle and both hindquarters for the 4 parcels and all the meat from the forequarters for the stuffing. To bone the hindquarters in one piece, locate the side on which the thigh bone is closer to the surface and cut through the meat to expose the bone. With short sharp strokes scraping against the bone, cut the meat from the bone. Cut around the joints, then scrape the meat away from the leg bone and pull it free. Pull out as many of the white tendons as possible.

POTATO AND ONION GRATIN WITH RED WINE

Gratin de pommes de terre et d'oignons au vin rouge

SERVES 4

60g/2oz/4 tbsp butter
2 onions (about 250g/¹/₂lb), peeled and
thinly sliced
250ml/8fl oz/1 cup red burgundy wine,
such as Irancy
salt and pepper
750g/1/¹/₂lb potatoes
1 tsp chopped fresh thyme leaves,
or ¹/₄ tsp dried thyme
2 bay leaves
250ml/8fl oz/1 cup chicken or veal stock

Melt half the butter in a heavy saucepan and cook the
onions over low heat, stirring frequently, for 10 minutes.
Add the wine and continue cooking, stirring occasionally,
until most of the wine has evaporated and the onions are
completely wilted and caramelized, about 15 minutes.
Season with salt and pepper.

Peel the potatoes and slice them thinly, using a mandoline slicer or food processor. Blot on paper towels, but do not rinse. Arrange half the potato slices overlapping in an even layer in the bottom of a generously buttered 30cm / 12 inch oval gratin dish. Season with salt and pepper, spread the onions over the potato layer, sprinkle the herbs on evenly and arrange the remaining potato slices on top in the same manner. Season with salt and pepper, dot with the remaining butter, and tuck a bay leaf in each end. Pour over the stock and cover the dish with foil. Bake in the middle of a preheated 190°C / 375°F / gas mark 5 oven. Remove the foil cover after 30 minutes and continue baking, near the top of the oven if possible, until well browned, about 15-20 minutes longer. Serve from the baking dish.

Note: It is possible to use stock made from bouillon cubes for this recipe, but use less salt for seasoning.

BITTER CHOCOLATE WAFERS WITH ALMOND PRALINE CREAM

Fines feuilles de chocolat amer et crème légère pralinée

SERVES 4

FOR THE CHOCOLATE WAFERS
3 egg yolks
60g/2oz/5 tbsp granulated sugar
30g/1oz/4 tbsp plain (all-purpose) flour
250ml/8fl oz/1 cup milk
100g/3½oz good quality plain (semi-sweet) chocolate, chopped
15g/½oz/2 tbsp cocoa powder

FOR THE PRALINE CREAM
60g/2oz whole unblanched almonds
60g/2oz/5 tbsp granulated sugar
250ml/8fl oz/1 cup whipping cream

FOR THE PRALINE CUSTARD SAUCE
250ml/8fl oz/1 cup milk
3 egg yolks
60g/2oz/5 tbsp granulated sugar
few drops vanilla essence (extract)
15g/½oz/1tbsp praline paste (made for the praline cream, above)

For the chocolate wafers, make a pastry cream. In a medium bowl, whisk the egg yolks with the sugar until slightly thickened, then whisk in the flour until smooth. Bring the milk to a boil and pour a little of the boiling milk into the egg yolks, whisking constantly to avoid forming lumps of cooked egg. Gradually whisk in the remaining milk, then pour it all back into the saucepan. Cook over moderate heat for 4-5 minutes, whisking constantly, until the mixture is smooth and thick and has come back to a boil. Add the chopped chocolate to the hot pastry cream and stir until completely melted. Sift in the cocoa powder and mix until completely smooth.

Preheat the oven to 200°C/400°F/gas mark 6. Place a teaspoon of the chocolate pastry cream batter on a non-stick baking sheet, and spread with the back of a spoon or a pastry brush to form a very thin round just over 7.5cm/ 3 inches in diameter. Continue with more batter, spacing them a few inches apart for easier removal. Bake the wafers in the preheated oven for about 10 minutes. (Bake some test wafers first to get the timing exactly right for your oven. The wafers will appear shiny and feel supple and leathery at this stage; they will become crisp and delicate when cool.) Remove from the oven and stamp each wafer with a 7.5-cm/3-inch pastry cutter to make perfect circles. Remove with a spatula to cool on a wire rack. Repeat to make 20 perfect wafers.

For the praline cream, make a praline paste (also used in the sauce). Combine the almonds and sugar in a copper sugar pan or a small heavy saucepan and cook over moderately high heat, stirring often until the sugar melts. Continue cooking, stirring occasionally, until the the mixture reaches a medium caramel and the almonds begin to pop. Take care, as this mixture is extremely hot. Remove from the heat and pour the caramel and nuts onto a lightly oiled baking sheet or marble slab and leave to cool completely. Using a rolling pin or mallet, break the cold caramel into small pieces, put in a food processor, and reduce to a paste. Reserve 1 tbsp of the praline paste for the custard sauce and set aside the remainder to flavour the praline cream.

To make the custard sauce, bring the milk to a boil in a heavy saucepan. Beat the egg yolks with the sugar in a

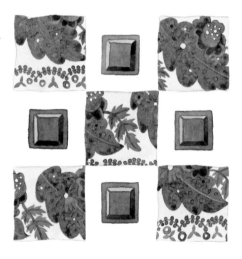

medium bowl until thick and pale, about 2 minutes. Whisk the milk into the egg yolk mixture, then pour it all back into the saucepan and and cook over a moderately low heat, stirring constantly with a wooden spoon, until the custard has thickened and will coat the back of a spoon. To test, remove the spoon and draw a line across the back with a finger: it should remain and not begin to fill in. Stir in the vanilla essence (extract) and 1 tbsp of the praline paste. Cool to room temperature, then refrigerate until needed, at least 1 hour.

To assemble the dessert, dilute the remaining praline cream with 2-3 tbsp of the whipping cream and stir until smooth. Whip the remaining cream until it forms stiff peaks and carefully fold in the diluted praline mixture until completely incorporated. On each of 4 dessert plates, put 5 spoonfuls of the cream close together in a ring in the centre of the plates. Arrange 1 wafer between each mound of praline cream, standing the wafers almost vertically to create a 'windmill' pattern. Pour a ribbon of the custard sauce around the rim of each plate and serve immediately.

Note: Praline paste is sometimes available commercially. Use 1 tbsp in the custard sauce and 5 tbsp in the cream.

CALF'S LIVER WITH POACHED EGG AND RED WINE SAUCE

Foie de veau et oeuf de poule en meurette

SERVES 4

90g/3oz/6 tbsp butter
2 onions, peeled and thinly sliced (about
250g/½lb)
500ml/16fl oz/2 cups red burgundy
wine, such as Irancy
salt and pepper
2 large shallots, peeled and finely chopped
500ml/16fl oz/2 cups chicken stock
4 very fresh eggs
3 tablespoons red wine vinegar
250g/½lb calf's liver, trimmed and cut
in slices 1cm/³⁄₈ inch thick

Melt 1 tbsp of the butter in a heavy saucepan and cook the onions over low heat, stirring frequently, for 10 minutes. Add 125ml/4fl oz/½ cup of the wine and continue cooking, stirring occasionally, until the wine has nearly evaporated and the onions are complerely wilted and lightly caramelized, about 10 minutes. Season with salt and pepper and keep warm.

Melt 1 tbsp of the butter in a small saucepan and cook the shallots for 2-3 minutes until softened. Add the remainder of the wine and boil until it has nearly all evaporated. Add the stock and continue boiling until it is reduced by half. Whisk in all but 1 tbsp of the remaining butter. Season to taste and keep the sauce warm.

Break the eggs into small dishes. Heat 1 litre / 1²/₃ pints / 1 quart water until barely simmering (just trembling, not realy moving). Add the vinegar and slide the eggs in one at a time. Poach the eggs for 4 minutes, remove with a slotted spoon and drain. Trim off any trailing egg white.

Remove any membrane from the liver, season on both sides and cut into 12 or 16 squares or diamond-shaped pieces. Heat the remaining 1 tbsp of butter in a heavy frying pan until foamy. Add the liver and cook about 1 minute on each side, turning once.

To serve, arrange a bed of onions in the centre of 4 warm plates. Put a poached egg on top and surround with the cooked liver, dividing the components evenly. Pour a little sauce over, and pass any remaining sauce.

Notes: The onion marmalade can be made ahead. Reheat for serving. The eggs may be poached ahead and kept in cold water until needed. Reheat in barely simmering water for 1 minute, and drain well before serving. Perforated egg poaching cups, if available, will help to keep the eggs shapely.

If preferred, to simplify the dish and serve as a main course, omit the poached eggs, and use double the quantity of liver, leaving it in large slices. Cook as above and serve with the onion marmalade.

WILD DUCK WITH
BRUSSELS SPROUTS

Canard sauvage à l'embeurée de choux de Bruxelles

SERVES 4

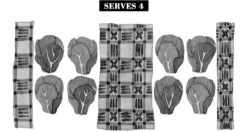

350g/³/₄lb Brussels sprouts
4 wild ducks, dressed and drawn
salt and pepper
90g/3oz/6 tbsp butter
375ml/12fl oz/1¹/₂ cups duck, game bird
or brown chicken stock
carrot flans, for serving (see page 88)

Cut off the stems and remove the leaves from the Brussels
sprouts. Cook the leaves in a large quantity of boiling
salted water until bright green and just tender. Drain and
refresh in cold water to stop the cooking and set the
colour.

Preheat the oven to 230°C/450°F/gas mark 8. Wipe
the ducks, season them inside and out with salt and pepper, and truss them. Smear about 1 tbsp of the butter over
the skin of each bird and put in a roasting pan. Roast the
ducks for 4 minutes breast side up and 6 minutes on each
leg, basting them each time they are turned. Remove from

the oven and allow the birds to rest for 10 minutes. Cut down each side of the breastbone to remove the breasts from the ducks in one piece and keep warm.

To make the sauce, chop the carcases and sauté in a heavy saucepan in 1 tbsp of the fat from the roasting pan. Add the stock and boil to reduce by about half. Strain and degrease the sauce.

Melt 2 tbsp of butter and reheat the Brussels sprouts. Season to taste with salt and pepper. Reheat the duck breasts for about 3 minutes in the hot oven or in the sauce. Arrange a bed of Brussels sprout leaves on each plate and lay 2 duck breasts on top. Pour a little sauce on top and pass the remainder. Serve with the carrot flans.

Note: If preferred, use only 2 wild ducks and serve 1 breast and 1 leg per person.

CARROT FLANS
Petites timbales de carottes

SERVES 4

350g/³/₄lb carrots, peeled and sliced
2 eggs
60ml/2fl oz/¹/₂ cup whipping cream
salt and pepper
¹/₂ tsp grated nutmeg
pinch of ground coriander

Cook the carrots in a large quantity of boiling salted water until soft. Drain well and purée in a food processor. Add the eggs and cream. Season with salt and pepper, nutmeg and coriander. Divide the mixture among 4 lightly buttered 125ml/4oz/¹/₂ cup ramekins and place them in a baking dish.

Pour boiling water into the baking dish to come halfway up the sides of the ramekins. Bake in a preheated 175°C/350°F/gas mark 4 oven until the flans are set and a knife inserted in the middle comes out clean, about 20 minutes.

Note: If preferred, omit the eggs and cream and serve the carrot purée on its own instead of making flans. Return to the saucepan to reheat and beat in about 30g/1oz/2 tbsp butter. Season to taste with salt and pepper and spoon into oval shapes for serving.

WARM CANDIED GRAPEFRUIT CREPES WITH GRAPEFRUIT SORBET

Petites crêpes et pamplemousse en chaud-froid

SERVES 4

2 large grapefruits, about 450g/1lb each
60g/2oz/5 tbsp granulated sugar

FOR THE CREPES
125g/4oz/1 cup plain (all-purpose) flour
15g/1 tbsp granulated sugar
pinch of salt
2 eggs
1 egg yolk
250ml/8fl oz/1 cup milk, or more
45g/1½oz/3 tbsp butter

FOR THE SORBET
500ml/16fl oz/2 cups freshly squeezed
grapefruit juice (from about 2 large grapefruits)
juice of ½ lemon
75g/2½ oz/6 tbsp granulated sugar
(approx)

To make the sorbet, combine the grapefruit juice, lemon juice and sugar in a saucepan. Bring to a boil, stirring to dissolve the sugar. Taste and add more sugar, if needed. Boil for 1 minute, remove from the heat and transfer to a shallow bowl. Let stand to cool, then refrigerate until cold. Pour the syrup into an ice cream machine and freeze according to manufacturer's instructions. (Alternatively, freeze the sweetened fruit juice mixture in a shallow tray or baking dish until nearly set, cut into small pieces and whip in a food processor or using and electric mixer until smooth. If wished, repeat the process several times for a more unctious consistency.)

To make the crêpes, put the flour, sugar and salt in a mixing bowl and make a well in the centre. Add the eggs, egg yolk, and a little of the milk to the well and whisk to mix the eggs. Keep whisking in small circles, drawing in the flour a little at a time. Add the milk gradually, still whisking in the centre and incorporating the flour slowly until a smooth batter has formed. Heat the butter until fragrant and light nutty brown. Cool slightly and whisk into the batter. Cover and leave to rest for $^{1}/_{2}$-4 hours.

When ready to cook the crêpes, whisk the batter and add a little more milk until it has the consistency of whipping cream. Heat a small crêpe pan or non-stick frying pan with a bottom diameter of 13cm/5 inches and brush the surface with a little butter. Pour in a small ladleful of batter (about 30ml/2 tbsp), tilting the pan at the same time to distribute it evenly. Cook gently 1-2 minutes, until the edges are brown. Turn over, using a spatula or your fingers, and cook 1 minute more. Slide the crêpe on to a plate and repeat with the remaining batter to make 20 crêpes, brushing the pan with butter as needed. Keep the crêpes warm.

With a small knife or vegetable peeler, pare the zest from both grapefruits, taking care to avoid the white pith. With a large knife, cut the zest into fine julienne strips. Blanch the zest in a small pan of boiling water. When it comes back to a boil, drain the zest, and refresh in cold water. Working over a bowl to catch the juice, pare away all the white pith and membrane from the grapefruits and cut out the segments from between the membranes. Squeeze the juice from the membranes after removing the segments. Pour the juice into a measuring container. Cover the segments and refrigerate. Add water if necessary to make 175ml/6fl oz/$^{3}/_{4}$ cup and combine with the sugar in a saucepan. Bring to a boil, stirring to dissolve the sugar, and add the blanched zest. Lower the heat and simmer for about 20 minutes until the liquid has reduced to a few spoonfuls of syrup and the zest is translucent and tender. Spread the zest on a sheet of greaseproof or waxed paper and set aside.

To assemble the dessert, reserve 4 pinches of candied zest for decoration, and divide the remainder among the warm crêpes, sprinkling a little over the surface of each, then folding the crêpe into quarters. Keep warm while folding the remaining crêpes. On each of 4 large plates, arrange 5 folded crêpes in a circle. Place 2-3 small scoops of grapefruit sorbet in the centre and top with the reserved zest. Arrange the grapefruit segments around the edge, dividing them evenly, and serve immediately.

Index